new skin

AF624604

Amanda Jane

BookLeaf Publishing

Presentation by *BookLeaf Publishing*

Web: www.bookleafpub.com

E-mail: info@bookleafpub.com

ISBN: 9789357445085

First edition 2022

DEDICATION

for lots of people, you know who you are and if you have to ask it's not you

nice

"Be nice".

Not
Inconvenient,
Compliant,
Easy.

lines

The concept of letting something happen to you negates the possibility that it should not have happened in the first place.
It means the question is not will this happen but how can I act when it does.
You know people cross lines so you keep redrawing them but the more common something is the closer you draw those lines to yourself, the further they get pushed.
And then by the time something does make it across it feels like the distance between what you were okay with and what you are not is too small to be justified.
So you turn it on yourself and either start slowly drawing them further away or stop drawing them altogether.

sickly sweet

i thought that i was stupid that i was incomplete
hot glue and frayed ribbons trying desperately to be neat
i remember through frosted windows
condensation from the heat
far too scared to wipe away the fog of sickly sweet

flies

Flies land on my skin like a carcass
not all of me knows I'm alive.
But the rest I can see through stained glass
far more vibrant than the pieces inside.

inhale exhale

inhale exhale.
place the sharpest point at your sternum.
inhale exhale.
deliberately drag down.
slit open your chest.
put down the object this is no longer precise.
inhale exhale.
make your fingers tear your thick skin
widen. open. expose.
inhale exhale.
pull at your ribs.
break them open.
feel them snap and snag your edges.
inhale exhale.
your heart she beats furiously.
echoing into the newly excavated space.
she's terrified
she's terrified of you
and she's never been this exposed without it
hurting.
inhale exhale.
let your fingers wander through the rot.
trace the scars.
feel the hurt through the tissue.
read the insults engraved inside your veins.

inhale exhale.
you've protected yourself violently.
tell her you're sorry.
greet her as a friend.
inhale exhale.
yes it hurts.
of course it hurts.
but this is release not rot.
inhale exhale.
show her.
show her that even with the object by your side
even with a clear shot even with the gnawing
idea you won't take her.
inhale exhale.
witness any carnage
admire what you've discarded
inhale exhale.
you've torn yourself open to seal yourself up.
inhale exhale.
close your chest.
leave the cracks.
inhale exhale.
if she protests
if the cracks scare her then say "but my friend
how else can light get through"
inhale exhale.
inhale exhale.
inhale exhale.

i'll be the dog

I want what wants me
There’s two things that haunt me
There’s five words I won’t speak
I’m too dry to come clean

Fake grass and gold trees
Tall rooms and old knees
You'd never speak up
It’s dismissed with bad luck

Dance till your sober and shake till you’re dry
I’ll be the dog if you leave me a life

circles

I'm a better listener than a talker
When I do talk I talk in circles
I repeat my sentences with minor edits,
slight variations,
rewording,
saying the same things instead of saying nothing
I talk in circles and I get embarrassed by the
shapes they make

bandage

is your sense of self to elusive
is your mistake too big to hide
is the weight of what you had to bandage
ready to release what's inside?

spiralling

I don't want to watch things get worse
I don't want to watch us shove the blame around and continue to do nothing
I don't want to watch the slow dissolution of the social structures underpinning our lives
I don't want to enjoy life because I don't want to miss it
I don't want 8 years
I want the illusion of forever
I want the possibility of younger generations
I want so viscerally to see a future but I cannot envision one longer than 48 hours at a time
I cannot hear anything except "you missed it"
I cannot think anything expect "you're stupid to try"
I cannot see anything except warning signs that I can do nothing about
The insignificance of my life is either hopelessly debilitating or recklessly liberating
The thought of planning ahead for my little life seems trite
The weight of uncertainty keeps me smothered in place so I choose to focus on the advertised certainty of our impending demise to at least bring structure and excuse my feelings

I'm tired but I'm awake
I'm trying but I'm aware
I'm too old but I'm too young
I'm too afraid to feel happy because it's fleeting
I'm too afraid to feel sad because it's not
I'm terrified that in the cyclical nature of our
feelings mine will end on a low point
I'm embarrassed that my concerns have begun to
centre around myself
Im scared
I thought there was more time
I'm sad
For the people who've built nice lives
I'm angry
That I spent so much of mine feeling wrong
I'm too much so I try to stay distracted because
one of the hardest parts of any difficult thing is
the awareness of it
Our house is on fire and most of us are still
trying to decorate

undecided

We are presented with the choice to try and do
better or to embrace extinction

And if this choice were mine I can't say what I'd
pick

I can't say I believe in our ability to co exist
I can't say I think better days are coming
I can't say we aren't horrible to each other and
to ourselves
I can't say we haven't pillaged our only
surroundings

But I can hope that enough other people would
choose to try and make the idea of hope seem
like less of a delusion to us undecided

new skin

new skin
old flesh
white hot
deep breaths
beat loud
no drum
re-run
day one

too tall

i wished i was taller
i wished like Alice i could grow to the size of
something bigger than an adult
drink me
eat me
just don't treat me like the child i'm not
i wished i looked as old as i felt
as old as i was treated
as old as i maybe should have been
i wished i was taller
but now im far too tall for how old i feel

some time

i look at my hands and they don't feel like mine
if my days were worth money they'd cost me a
dime
i check every corner insisting it's fine
i listen for sounds i haven't heard in some time.

i forgot

i forgot i was alive
every breath every second did not feel like mine
my hands felt like others losing the concept of
time
i looked back at a face that kept repeating "I'm
fine"
and liking the mirror felt akin to a crime
i forgot i was alive
or maybe i never thought about it in the first
place
i was trained for the race
i mastered the "brave face"
i resigned to the steady pace
i forgot i was alive
and it almost didn't matter
i climbed a precarious ladder
and couldn't decide between the former or the
latter
i forgot i was alive
i think maybe i never knew
but i hope next time i see a mirror i can say "it's
you"

swimming

I drowned myself and called it strength
I kept pushing myself deeper thinking it would teach me how to swim
I tried it grow gills instead of heading to shore and became frustrated when my body wouldn't evolve into conditions it wasn't built for
The idea of floating felt easier than trying to stand but I kept forgetting that the water wasn't still either
It was simply familiar
I knew how to tread water
I knew how to hold my breath
I felt a sense of accomplishment in my exhaustion because i thought it meant i was working hard enough
Could i go deeper?
Could i hold my breath longer?
Probably
But just because I've come up for air every time so far doesn't mean I haven't found my limits

but i seldom take it

Breathe in the in between
Sit in the unknown but try not to succumb to it
Stay yourself once you know who that is and
love that it changes
Get out of your own head to let others in not to
keep yourself out
Be proud of yourself for what you've
accomplished
Be honest about what you have yet to

on my terms

I thought about it
I entertained it
I let it perform in my head a saga of four acts,
alternate timelines, a set of options, a wide
variety of tales varying from severe to mundane
But every act that played left me with the same
feelings
Almost all of which were violently contradictory
How can I keep the spark contained
How can I swim against the current
How can I feel responsible and reckless
How can I return when all you want from me is
pieces that I can't give anymore

thoughts

If I'm not my thoughts what am I
Am I a collection of what people think of me
What they perceive
What I choose to show
Am I a fragment of every person I've met
A patchwork personality
A mosaic of moments
Am I a reaction to my surroundings
A response rather than an action
A passive ideation of missed opportunities
Or
Does what I am not matter
Does what I do say more than the onslaught of opinions others have of me and that I have of myself
Do I limit my actions by being consumed by the possibility of their consequences
Do I feel safety in the anticipation of fear
I don't know
Because I am not my thoughts

there are some people

There are some people I miss more than I
remember and some people I remember more
than I miss
I wish I could switch the two, be the glue, see it
through, cut myself in two
one to remember
And one to miss
permanent agony and temporary bliss
I've split myself before and I can do it again
But the reunion each time makes it harder to be
friends
each piece feels so different when they start to
blend and I've employed haphazard ways to
attempt to mend the pieces I remember and the
ideas I miss
The places I don't go to
The parts kissed by a fist
The band-aid jokes
The missed high-notes
The too-young folks
The old for your age

The message on the page I didn't use, expunged
the fuse, waited for the bruise instead of what I
thought I wanted to do
there are some people
Some people I quite like to see
Some people I talk to till 3:00
Some people who have felt better than bliss
And there are some people that I will always
miss.

i used to

I used to get excited for things
I made playlists for events
I packed for trips in my mind
I researched things I wanted to do and places I
wanted to go
I got excited for things
I mapped out their possibilities
I charted their courses
I wanted to remember details that hadn't
happened yet
So I'm making a to do list
For being excited
make a playlist
look up photos
read about places
pack for fun
talk about what you want to do
think about good things that might happen as
opposed to anticipating the bad
is it risky absolutely
is it worth it I don't know
but I'd rather deal with disappointment should it
arise than plan for it's certainty

i'm certain i don't know

I didn't realize it was ending
In fact I was certain it was beginning
I thought I had yet to even start
So when I thought it stopped
I thought I missed it
I thought I waited too long
I decided it was over
And I was right it wasn't starting at all
something else was ending
Times that didn't feel like they counted because
I didn't feel real yet
Times I didn't think about because it was easier
if they didn't exist
Times that were far more important than the idea
of the future I thought I missed
Something was ending
As all things do
Eventually, exquisitely, and occasionally
unexpectedly
And now that part's ended I feel certain of very
little and I know even less
But now I'm certain I don't know

www.ingramcontent.com/pod-product-compliance
Lightning Source LLC
Chambersburg PA
CBHW051718130826
49812CB00034B/1235